from SEA TO SHINING SEA
MINNESOTA

By Dennis Brindell Fradin and Judith Bloom Fradin

CONSULTANTS

Ellen B. Green, St. Paul
Robert L. Hillerich, Ph.D., Professor Emeritus, Bowling Green State University;
Consultant, Pinellas County Schools, Florida

CHILDRENS PRESS ®
CHICAGO

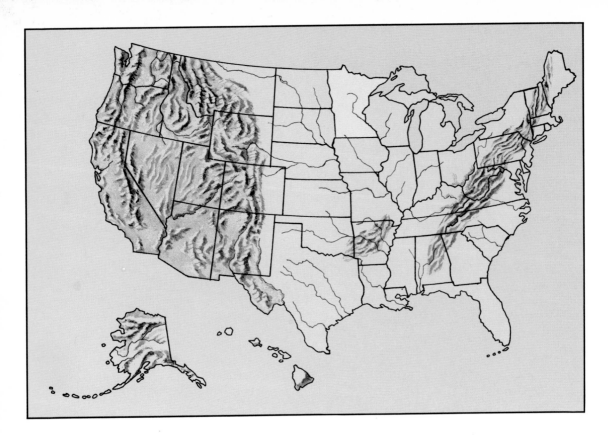

Minnesota is one of the twelve states in the region called the Midwest. The other Midwest states are Illinois, Indiana, Iowa, Kansas, Michigan, Missouri, Nebraska, North Dakota, Ohio, South Dakota, and Wisconsin.

For our daughter Diana, a beautiful state for a beautiful girl

Front cover picture: Landmark Center, Minneapolis; page 1: misty sunrise over farmland near East Grand Forks; back cover: Palisade Head and Lake Superior

Project Editor: Joan Downing
Design Director: Karen Kohn
Typesetting: Graphic Connections, Inc.
Engraving: Liberty Photoengraving

Library of Congress Cataloging-in-Publication Data

Fradin, Dennis B.
  Minnesota / by Dennis Brindell Fradin & Judith Bloom
Fradin.
    p.   cm. — (From sea to shining sea)
  Includes index.
  ISBN 0-516-03823-0
    1. Minnesota—Juvenile literature. [1. Minnesota.]
I. Fradin, Judith Bloom. II. Title. III. Series: Fradin,
Dennis B. From sea to shining sea.
F606.3.F69   1995   94-35021
977.6—dc20   CIP
                                               AC

Table of Contents

A winter sleigh ride in Copas

INTRODUCING THE GOPHER STATE

Before Alaska became a state in 1959, Minnesota was the farthest north of the states.

Minnesota is a far northern state in the midwestern United States. It is known for its woods and waters. The state's name means "cloud-reflecting water" in the Dakota Indian language. Minnesota is often called the "Land of Sky-Blue Waters." Another nickname is "Land of 10,000 Lakes." But Minnesota's main nickname is the "Gopher State." This came from an 1859 cartoon. Some men wanted a railroad to go through Minnesota. They were shown as gophers wearing top hats.

Today, Minnesota is a giant milk, hog, turkey, corn, and sugar-beet producer. It leads the country at mining iron ore. Minnesota factories make computers, breakfast cereals, tape, and farm equipment. Minnesotans are among the best-educated and healthiest people in the United States.

The Gopher State is also special in other ways. Where was "Peanuts" comic-strip creator Charles Schulz born? Where were snowmobiles and waterskiing invented? Where was the world's first open-heart surgery performed? The answer to these questions is: Minnesota!

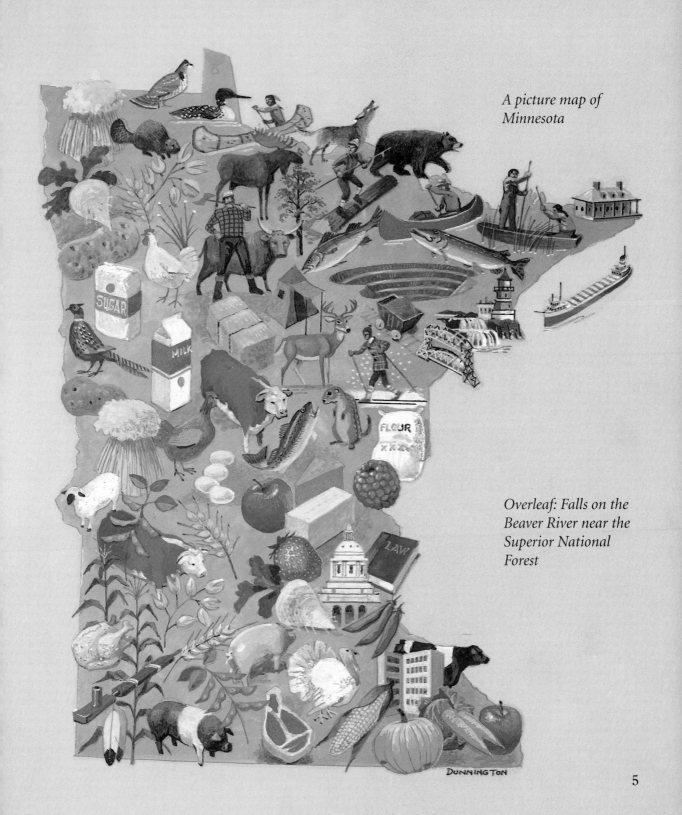

A picture map of
Minnesota

Overleaf: Falls on the
Beaver River near the
Superior National
Forest

DUNNINGTON

The Land of 10,000 Lakes

THE LAND OF 10,000 LAKES

Lake Superior is one of the five Great Lakes at the United States-Canada border.

Minnesota covers 84,402 square miles in the Midwest. It is the twelfth-largest of the fifty states. But of the twelve midwestern states, Minnesota is the biggest. Four Midwest states border Minnesota. North Dakota and South Dakota lie to the west. Iowa is Minnesota's southern neighbor. Lake Superior and the state of Wisconsin are to the east. The country of Canada is to the north. Minnesota's Northwest Angle points into Canada. Minnesota lies the farthest north of the Lower 48 states. That is why Minnesota is called the "North Star State."

Southern Minnesota is mostly plains. These flat to gently hilly lands reach into northwest Minnesota. The Superior Upland covers the rest of northern Minnesota. This land is mountainous in places. Minnesota's highest point is there. Eagle Mountain stands 2,301 feet above sea level.

LAKES AND RIVERS

Lake Superior splashes against northeast Minnesota. Covering 32,000 square miles, it is the world's

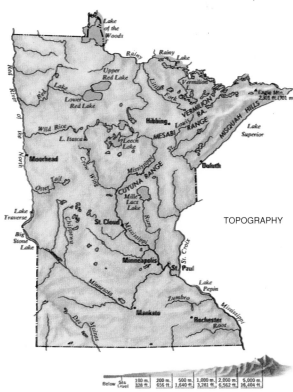

TOPOGRAPHY

Below Sea Level	100 m. 328 ft.	200 m. 656 ft.	500 m. 1,640 ft.	1,000 m. 3,281 ft.	2,000 m. 6,562 ft.	5,000 m. 16,404 ft.

largest freshwater lake. Red Lake is the largest lake within Minnesota. It covers 430 square miles in northern Minnesota. Lake of the Woods and Rainy Lake are also big lakes. Minnesota and Canada share them. Altogether, Minnesota has more than 15,000 lakes.

The country's longest river begins at northwest Minnesota's Lake Itasca. The Mississippi River curls southeast across Minnesota. It then forms part of the border with Wisconsin. The Minnesota River flows across southern Minnesota. The St. Croix River forms the rest of the border with Wisconsin. The Red River separates Minnesota from North

Left: Lake Superior shoreline

Birch trees in Split Rock State Park

Timber wolf

Dakota. The St. Louis and Crow Wing are other rivers in Minnesota.

WOODS AND WILDLIFE

Woodlands cover over one-third of Minnesota. The Norway pine is the state tree. Birches, spruces, oaks, and maples also grow in Minnesota. The state also has 14,000 square miles of wetlands. Minnesota's state flower is the pink and white lady's slipper. It grows in swamps and damp woods. Wild rice is the state grain. It grows in shallow Minnesota waters.

White-tailed deer, black bears, and moose roam Minnesota's woods. About 2,000 timber wolves live there, too. Only Alaska has more timber wolves. In places, bobcats prowl about after rabbits and squirrels. Foxes, otters, raccoons, woodchucks, and weasels also live in Minnesota. So do gophers, for whom the state is nicknamed.

Ducks are found on Minnesota lakes. Nearly 600 pairs of bald eagles nest in the state. Owls, sparrows, pheasants, and woodpeckers are other Minnesota birds. The common loon is the state bird. It dives for fish on Minnesota lakes. The walleye is the state fish. Northern pike, bass, and trout are also found in Minnesota waters. So are huge fish

called muskellunges. "Muskies" can grow big enough to eat ducks.

CLIMATE

Minnesotans say they have two seasons, "shovel and swat." They shovel snow during their long, cold winters. They swat mosquitoes during the summers. Snowfalls over 4 inches are common from November through April. About twice a year, snowstorms driven by high winds strike. These are called blizzards. Winter temperatures often dip below 0 degrees Fahrenheit.

Summer temperatures are often a pleasant 70 degrees Fahrenheit. Yet, temperatures sometimes top 90 degrees Fahrenheit. Thunderstorms with hail are common from May to September. Tornadoes sometimes whirl down on Minnesota in the warmer months, too.

A springtime picture of reeds in Nelson Pool, Sherburne National Wildlife Refuge

On some days, International Falls, in northern Minnesota, has the nation's coldest winter weather outside Alaska.

Overleaf: Harvesting in the Red River Valley, 1910

11

From Ancient Times Until Today

FROM ANCIENT TIMES UNTIL TODAY

About 2 million years ago, the Ice Age began. Glaciers covered most of Minnesota. Only the southeast corner was free of these ice masses. As the glaciers moved, they spread rich soil. They also carved holes in the ground. When the Ice Age ended, the holes filled with water. They became Minnesota's lakes.

AMERICAN INDIANS

The first people reached Minnesota more than 12,000 years ago. These ancient Indians are sometimes called the Big Game people. They hunted large animals. These included elephantlike animals called mammoths and mastodons.

By 5,000 years ago, the Indians had carved pictures on rocks (petroglyphs). In southwestern Minnesota, the Jeffers Petroglyphs have carvings of people and animals. The Indians also mined pipestone in southwest Minnesota. They carved peace pipes from this soft stone.

Later, two major Indian groups lived in Minnesota. The Dakota were there first. They lived

The Jeffers Petroglyphs were carved by Plains Indians.

in Minnesota's northern and eastern woods. The Dakota built bark homes called wigwams. When traveling, they lived in tepees. These were tents made from animal skins. The Dakota hunted deer and buffalo with bows and arrows. They grew corn and beans. They also fished.

The Ojibway moved into Minnesota in the late 1600s. They, too, lived in wigwams. The Ojibway made swift birch-bark canoes. They made snowshoes for winter travel. Like the Dakota, the Ojibway hunted and fished. Both tribes gathered wild rice.

The Dakota (above) were also called the Sioux. The Ojibway were also called the Chippewa.

A framework for a birch-bark wigwam

FRENCH AND BRITISH TRADERS

The first Europeans known to reach Minnesota were French fur traders. Around 1660, Pierre Radisson and Médard Chouart, Sieur des Groseilliers, came from Canada. They received furs from Dakota Indians along Lake Superior.

In 1679, Daniel Greysolon, Sieur Du Luth, crossed Lake Superior in a canoe. He landed where the city of Duluth now stands. Du Luth claimed the land for France. He also made friends with the Indians. In 1680, Father Louis Hennepin traveled up the Mississippi River. For a time, he traveled with some Dakota Indians. While he was with them,

Hennepin saw a beautiful waterfall. It was on the Mississippi River. He named it the Falls of St. Anthony. The city of Minneapolis began at that falls.

Other Frenchmen, called voyageurs, came in canoes. They worked for trading companies. The voyageurs brought tools and clothes for traders to exchange for beaver and other furs. The traders built posts along Minnesota's rivers. There the French and Indians met to do business. Pierre Le Sueur built an outpost near what is now Red Wing in 1695. He built another trading post near what is now Mankato in 1700.

In 1763, England gained control of Canada and the Great Lakes country from France. In 1783, many independent English fur traders formed the North West Company. The partners met each summer at Grand Portage.

Voyageurs like this costumed guide at Grand Portage National Monument worked for the trading companies. Voyageur is a French word meaning "traveler."

THE UNITED STATES GAINS CONTROL

In 1783, the United States gained control of England's Minnesota lands. Twenty years later, the United States bought France's land west of the Mississippi. This included western Minnesota. The United States flag then flew over all of Minnesota.

17

Members of the 5th U.S. Infantry were stationed at Fort Snelling.

A painting of St. Paul as it looked in 1855

In 1819, American soldiers began building Fort Snelling. A few families settled near the fort in 1821. They were the first non-Indian settlers to farm in Minnesota. In 1823, the first steamboat came up the Mississippi River. The *Virginia* had traveled to Fort Snelling from St. Louis, Missouri. Steamboats made it easier for people to reach Minnesota.

More settlers trickled into Minnesota during the 1830s and 1840s. Minneapolis and St. Paul were founded. They became known as the Twin Cities. The Mississippi River forms part of their boundary.

In 1848, some settlers met at the town of Stillwater. They asked the United States Congress to

make Minnesota a territory. In 1849, Congress created the Minnesota Territory. A year later, about 6,000 people lived in the territory. By 1858, that number had climbed to 150,000. This was more than enough people for statehood. Congress made Minnesota the thirty-second state on May 11, 1858. St. Paul became Minnesota's first and only capital.

Because the move for statehood started in Stillwater, that town is known as the "Birthplace of Minnesota."

The Civil War and the Dakota Wars

Minnesota entered the Union as a free state. The southern states allowed slavery. In 1861, southern guns fired on a Union fort off South Carolina. That marked the beginning of the Civil War (1861-1865). Minnesota was the first state to offer soldiers. About 20,000 Minnesotans served the North (Union). Slavery was one of the causes of the war. The northern victory in 1865 ended slavery in the United States.

During the Civil War, Minnesotans fought a war of their own. In the 1850s, the Dakota had sold their land to the United States. In return, the government was to give them food and supplies. During the Civil War, the government did not carry out its promise. The Indians then tried to hunt for food on settlers' land.

In August 1862, five settlers were killed. This started the Dakota wars of 1862. Chief Little Crow was talked into leading 1,500 Dakota warriors. They burned Minnesota towns and killed nearly 500 settlers. In September, soldiers led by Henry Sibley defeated the Dakota. The Indians were put on trial. Thirty-eight Dakota were hanged. Most of the others were driven out of Minnesota.

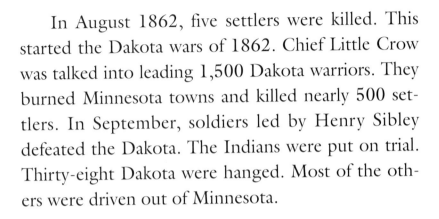

Sibley was Minnesota's first state governor (1858-1860).

LOGGING, FARMING, AND MINING

By the 1870s, railroads crisscrossed the state. They helped turn logging into a big Minnesota business. Lumberjacks chopped down trees by the thousands. The lumber went by train to other parts of the country. Minnesota wood helped build many United States cities.

But the logging companies cut down too many trees. They didn't plant new ones. Whole forests were destroyed. Poor safety practices made fire a problem, too. In 1894, a giant forest fire struck eastern Minnesota. Hinckley and several other towns burned. More than 400 people died in the Great Hinckley Fire.

In the late 1800s, western Minnesota was covered by huge wheat farms. By 1890, Minnesota led

In the 1870s, railroads were used to transport lumber and grain from Minnesota to other parts of the country.

the country at growing wheat. Mills along Minnesota rivers ground the wheat into flour. Much bread was made from the flour. Minnesota was called the "Bread Basket." The raising of dairy cattle gained importance, too. Butter was made from Minnesota milk. Some people called Minnesota the "Bread and Butter State."

Between 1884 and 1911, iron ore was found in northeastern Minnesota. The Vermilion Range produced the first ore in 1884. In the 1890s, the seven Merritt brothers found iron ore in the Mesabi Range. By 1900, the Mesabi Range was the coun-

In the 1870s and 1880s lumberjacks like these chopped down Minnesota trees by the thousands.

try's leading source of iron ore. Minnesota was the top iron-mining state. In 1911, more ore was found in the Cuyuna Range.

Logging, farming, and mining attracted new settlers. Many came from Germany, Norway, Ireland, and Sweden. Others arrived from Poland, the Yugoslavian states, Hungary, and Italy. By 1900, Minnesota's population was 1,751,394.

WORLD WARS, POLITICS, AND THE DEPRESSION

In 1917, the United States entered World War I (1914-1918). More than 123,000 Minnesotans served. Minnesota wheat and iron ore also helped the war effort. After the war, a movement for world

Secretary of State Frank C. Kellogg (third from right, in the front) witnessed President Coolidge signing the Kellogg-Briand Peace Pact in 1928. Kellogg won the 1929 Nobel Peace Prize for his work.

peace started. A Minnesotan, Frank B. Kellogg, was United States secretary of state. In 1928, he worked out the Kellogg-Briand Peace Pact. It tried to outlaw war.

Meanwhile, many Minnesota farmers and laborers were unhappy. The farmers felt that the railroads and banks were cheating them. Factory workers put in long hours for low pay. The Farmer-Labor party was formed by Minnesotans in 1918. This new political party worked on behalf of farmers and factory workers.

The Great Depression (1929-1939) brought hard times to Minnesota. Most iron miners lost

During the depression, these jobless men and farmers marched on the state capitol to plea for relief.

Two Farmer-Labor party governors followed Olson: Hjalmar Petersen (1936-1937) and Elmer Benson (1937-1939).

During World War II, this woman worked in the Twin Cities Ordnance Plant in Arden Hills.

their jobs. Prices for crops dropped. Factories closed. Floyd Olson served as Minnesota's governor during much of the depression (1931-1936). He was the first Farmer-Labor party governor. Olson started programs to help farmers keep their farms. Other actions included relief for the jobless.

World War II (1939-1945) helped end the depression. The United States entered the war in 1941. Minnesota's farmers, miners, and loggers helped the war effort. Minnesota's factories turned out parts for aircraft and ships. About 325,000 Minnesota men and women served in uniform.

RECENT CHANGES

Since the 1950s, Minnesota has gained nearly 1.5 million people. Thousands of black people and Asian people have moved to the state. The Twin Cities area has more than half of the state's population.

The Gopher State has begun new programs for its people in recent years. In 1987, the state started a school-choice program. It allows students to pick the school they want to attend. Also in 1987, Minnesota began "Second Chance." This program has brought thousands of dropouts back to high

school. Such programs make Minnesota a leader in education.

In 1992, Minnesota pioneered a new health-insurance program. It covers many jobless people and poor families.

Water pollution has been one of Minnesota's biggest problems. In the 1970s, Lake Superior became polluted. Waste from paper mills, taconite plants, and sewage entered the lake. Minnesota and Canada have worked together to clean Lake Superior. Their efforts have greatly improved its water. Farm and factory chemicals have entered other Minnesota streams and lakes. Minnesotans are working to clean them, too. They want their state always to be the Land of Sky-Blue Waters.

Yachts in the Knife River Marina on Lake Superior

Overleaf: Picking strawberries in Hastings

25

Minnesotans and Their Work

MINNESOTANS AND THEIR WORK

Minnesota has about 4.4 million people. More than 9 of 10 Minnesotans are white. Most of their families came from Germany, Norway, Ireland, and Sweden. About 100,000 Minnesotans are black. Another 20,000 are Hmong. They are Asian people from Laos. About 60,000 other Asians live in the state. About 55,000 Minnesotans have Hispanic (Spanish-speaking) backgrounds.

Minnesota is home to almost 50,000 American Indians. About 32,000 are Ojibway. Another 6,000 are Dakota. Minnesota has fourteen Indian reservations. American Indians also live in towns and cities throughout the state.

Minnesota is home to about 100,000 black people and about 80,000 Asians.

THEIR WORK

About 2.4 million Minnesotans have jobs. Almost 600,000 are service workers. These people include lawyers, computer repairers, and hotel workers. The University of Minnesota's hospital employs thousands of health-care workers. National Car Rental is based in Edina.

Some Minnesota Native Americans make handcrafted products.

A professor at Macalester College in St. Paul

Nearly 550,000 Minnesotans sell goods. Minneapolis is home to Dayton Hudson. This national department store chain includes Dayton's, Target, and Marshall Field's. Supervalu Stores, Inc., is a grocery chain. It is based near Minneapolis. The Twin Cities area is also home to Cargill. This huge firm distributes farm products worldwide.

About 500,000 Minnesotans make goods. Machinery is their top product. Control Data Systems and Cray Research make computers. Honeywell makes airplane and spacecraft equipment. Many Americans adjust the heat in their homes with Honeywell thermostats. Foods rank second among Minnesota products. Meat, flour, cereals, sugar, and canned and frozen vegetables lead the list. Butter and cheese are other important goods. Other Minnesotans make heart valves and pacemakers. Scotch™ tape and Post-It™ Notes are made by St. Paul's 3M Company.

Minnesota has about 360,000 government workers. They include letter carriers and teachers. Nearly 150,000 Minnesotans work for banks, insurance companies, and real estate companies. Another 100,000 work in transportation and related fields. Northwest Airlines is a leading world airline. It is based in Eagan, near the Twin Cities.

Since 1970, the number of Minnesota farms has dropped from 100,000 to 87,000. Yet, its 100,000 farmworkers still make Minnesota a top farming state. Minnesotans raise large numbers of dairy cows, hogs, turkeys, and beef cattle. Eggs and milk are other important farm goods. The Gopher State is the number-one state at growing sugar beets. Other crops include oats, soybeans, barley, corn, hay, wheat, and potatoes.

About 7,000 Minnesotans work in mining. Minnesota has led the country at mining iron ore since 1901. In the 1950s, a lower-quality iron ore began to be mined. It comes from a rock called taconite. A plant in Silver Bay removes the iron ore from the taconite. Clay, sand and gravel, and granite are also mined in Minnesota.

An open-pit iron-ore mine in Chisholm

Minnesota has about 5 million hogs. That is just over one per person. Minnesota farmers sell 40 million turkeys a year.

Overleaf: The Duluth Convention Center area at dusk

29

*A Trip Through
the Gopher State*

A Trip Through the Gopher State

Minnesota's woods and lakes supply a year-round playground. Minnesotans and visitors enjoy waterskiing, swimming, canoeing, fishing, and boating in the summers. In the winters, they go ice fishing, snowmobiling, and cross-country skiing. Ice-skating and hockey are popular, too. The Twin Cities and smaller towns add to the fun of a Minnesota visit.

Minnesota has 2,500 miles of cross-country ski trails.

The Twin Cities Area

Minneapolis means "city of water."

Minneapolis is the larger of the Twin Cities. With 363,383 people, it is also the state's largest city. This "City of Lakes" has eighteen lakes. Minneapolis also has two famous waterfalls. The soft limestone ledge under the Falls of St. Anthony has been reinforced with cement. Today, it looks more like a dam than a rushing waterfall. The 53-foot Minnehaha Falls is hidden among trees in Minnehaha Park.

Poet Henry Wadsworth Longfellow popularized Minnehaha Falls in The Song of Hiawatha. *A statue of Hiawatha, Longfellow's Indian hero, carrying his wife Minnehaha is at the falls.*

The state's tallest building is in Minneapolis. The fifty-seven-story IDS Tower is 775 feet high. The Guthrie Theater attracts playgoers from around

the world. The Minneapolis Institute of Arts is one of the country's great art museums. The Walker Art Center is a modern-art museum. The Minneapolis Sculpture Garden has wonderful outdoor sculpture.

Three major pro sports teams play in Minneapolis. The Minnesota Twins play baseball at the Hubert H. Humphrey Metrodome. The Twins won the 1987 and 1991 World Series. The Minnesota Vikings play football at the Metrodome. The Minnesota Timberwolves play basketball at Target Center.

Left: The giant Spoonbridge and Cherry sculpture in the Minneapolis Sculpture Garden was designed by Claes Oldenburg and Coosje van Bruggen.
Right: Nicollet Mall

The state capitol

The chamber of the House of Representatives

St. Paul is the state's second-biggest city. It has 272,235 people. St. Paul is also Minnesota's capital. Minnesota lawmakers meet in the state capitol. It has one of the world's largest self-supporting marble domes.

St. Paul also has many museums. Visitors can learn about the state's past at the Minnesota History Center. The Minnesota Children's Museum has exhibits on recycling paper and on Minnesota inventors. The Science Museum of Minnesota has an 82-foot-long skeleton of a Diplodocus. This was the longest dinosaur.

South of the Twin Cities is Fort Snelling. It has been restored to look like an 1820s fort. To the east is Sibley House. Built in 1835, it was Minnesota's first stone house. Henry H. Sibley lived in this Mendota home. He was Minnesota's first state governor. The Minnesota Zoo is at nearby Apple Valley. Nearly 500 kinds of animals live there.

South of Minneapolis is Bloomington. It is Minnesota's third-biggest city. Settled in 1843, Bloomington has grown to a city of 86,335. The Minnesota Valley National Wildlife Refuge is there. The United States has 500 national wildlife refuges. Bloomington's is one of the few found in a city. Murphy's Landing is in nearby Shakopee. People in costumes show what pioneer life was like.

SOUTHERN MINNESOTA HIGHLIGHTS

Northfield is south of the Twin Cities. In 1876, the Jesse James gang tried to rob a bank there. The townspeople opened fire on the gang. Jesse and his brother Frank James escaped. The rest of the gang were killed or captured. Each September, the shoot-out is reenacted in Northfield.

Lake Pepin is east of Northfield. This is a large pocket in the Mississippi River. Waterskiing was

The Diplodocus skeleton at the Science Museum of Minnesota

The Jesse James gang's Northfield bank robbery is reenacted every September.

invented at Lake Pepin in 1922. A motorboat pulled a young man balancing on skis.

Winona is farther south on the Mississippi. Garvin Heights is a 600-foot-high bluff in Winona. It offers a beautiful view of the river and the surrounding countryside. The Julius C. Wilkie Steamboat Center is docked at Winona. This replica of an old-time steamboat houses a museum about Mississippi River vessels.

West of Winona is Rochester. With 70,745 people, it is Minnesota's fifth-biggest city. Rochester was founded in 1854 as a stopping place for wagon

The Julius C. Wilkie Steamboat Center in Winona

The Mayo Clinic in Rochester

trains. Today, more than 300,000 patients stop there each year. They seek help at Rochester's Mayo Clinic. In 1889, Dr. William Worrall Mayo started the clinic. His sons William and Charles made it world famous. Mayowood was Dr. Charles Mayo's estate. Today, this home is open for public tours.

Mankato is northwest of Rochester. The town's name means "blue earth" in the Dakota language. Much blue clay is found along the riverbanks. The Blue Earth County Historical Museum is in Mankato. Visitors can see displays of pioneer clothing and tools. Each fall the Dakota hold a powwow at Mankato. Thousands of non-Indians attend the powwow, too. Indian foods are served. These include fry bread, buffalo stew, and wild-rice soup.

New Ulm is northwest of Mankato. German people began the town in 1854. New Ulm is known for its German craft shops, foods, and customs. A 45-foot-tall musical clock tower stands in New Ulm. It is called the Glockenspiel. The clock's toy musicians play three times each day.

Pipestone National Monument is near Minnesota's southwest corner. This land is sacred to many Indian tribes. They still dig soft, red sandstone here. The Indians make peace pipes and other objects from it.

CENTRAL MINNESOTA HIGHLIGHTS

St. Cloud is northwest of Minneapolis. Hard rock granite has long been quarried there. Visitors can learn about St. Cloud's granite industry at the Stearns County Heritage Center.

North of St. Cloud is Little Falls. Charles Lindbergh grew up there. He became a famous pilot. Charles A. Lindbergh State Park is just outside of town. Lindbergh's childhood home is in the park. It looks as it did in the early 1900s.

Brainerd is north of Little Falls. Children enjoy Brainerd's Paul Bunyan Amusement Center. This

In 1927, "Lucky Lindy" became the first pilot to fly nonstop across the Atlantic Ocean alone. The picture shows Lindbergh's boyhood home in Little Falls.

amusement park was named for the giant lumber-jack in tall tales. A huge talking statue of Bunyan greets each child by name. Lumbertown U.S.A. is near Brainerd. Its twenty-six buildings recreate an 1870s logging town.

Alexandria is southwest of Brainerd. The Kensington Runestone Museum is there. Visitors can see a stone with strange writing carved on it. The stone was overturned by a farmer in nearby Kensington in 1898. Some people believe the rune-stone was left by Vikings in 1362.

Fergus Falls is west of Alexandria. Its Otter Trail County Museum shows farm life of 100 years ago. An Indian home and an 1800s Main Street have also been rebuilt.

NORTHERN MINNESOTA

Moorhead is north of Fergus Falls. It lies along the Red River at the Minnesota-North Dakota border. Moorhead's Plains Art Museum has American Indian and West African artworks. The Heritage-Hjemkomst Interpretive Center has museums and shops. The center was named after a Viking ship. Visitors can view this replica of the *Hjemkomst*. It was built by Moorhead's Robert Asp. In 1982, the

The Kensington Runestone

Below: The Heritage-Hjemkomst Interpretive Center. Hjemkomst is a Norwegian word meaning "homecoming."

The Boundary Waters Canoe Area Wilderness north of Ely

Hjemkomst sailed 6,000 miles from Duluth to Bergen, Norway.

To the north is Thief River Falls. Its Friendship Garden honors the goodwill between the United States and Canada. The town is also famous for snowmobiles. The Arctic Cat is built and tested there. Farther north in Roseau, the first snowmobile was made in 1953. Today, Roseau's Polaris plant is the leading producer of snowmobiles.

Agassiz National Wildlife Refuge is between the two snowmobile towns. Timber wolves, golden eagles, and bald eagles can be seen there. The refuge's wolf pack is the only one in the United States outside Alaska. To the east is Voyageurs National Park. It is nearly midway along the border with Canada. The park was named for the French voyageurs. Today, park rangers guide trips in replicas of voyageurs' canoes.

Because of its shape, northeastern Minnesota is nicknamed the Arrowhead Country. Superior National Forest covers most of it. Ely is in the middle of this forest. The town has many stores with supplies for campers and canoeists. There are no roads north of Ely. To go farther north, visitors travel by canoe. They carry their canoes between the lakes. Those lakes are part of the Boundary Waters Canoe Area Wilderness. This is the country's first wilderness set aside for canoeing.

The North West Company's fur-trading post at Grand Portage has been rebuilt. This picture shows tables in the Great Hall covered with fur pelts and other items.

Grand Portage National Monument is at Minnesota's northeast tip. Long ago, traders exchanged goods at the North West Company's fur-trading post. The post has since been rebuilt. Costumed guides and workers take visitors back to the days of the voyageurs.

South along Lake Superior lies Duluth. By the late 1700s, it, too, was a fur-trading center. Today, with 85,493 people, Duluth is Minnesota's fourth-

Above: Ore boats at Duluth

Duluth and other Great Lakes ports are linked to the Atlantic Ocean by the St. Lawrence Seaway.

The Iron Man *statue at the Minnesota Museum of Mining in Chisholm*

largest city. Duluth's port is the country's busiest non-ocean port. Coal, iron ore, and wheat are shipped from Duluth. Close to the port is the Canal Park Marine Museum. Visitors can learn about shipwrecks and shipping on the Great Lakes. Glensheen stands on Duluth's Lake Superior shore. This thirty-nine-room mansion was built by Chester Congdon. He was a wealthy iron-mine owner.

Each January, a 500-mile sled-dog race begins and ends in Duluth. The John Beargrease Sled Dog Marathon runs from Duluth to Grand Portage and back. The winning musher earns about $10,000.

West of Duluth is the Iron Range. The iron-mining towns of Eveleth, Chisholm, and Hibbing stand close together. Taconite is mined at Eveleth. The town is home to the United States Hockey Hall of Fame. Hockey players from across the United States are honored there. The Minnesota Museum of Mining is at Chisholm. It has a restored iron-mining village. The *Iron Man* statue guards the museum's entrance. Ironworld USA is across from the museum. The history of iron mining is told there. Hibbing once had the world's largest open-pit iron mine. The Hull-Rust-Mahoning Mine was 3 miles long and over 500 feet deep. It has been filled with water and is now a lake.

To the southwest is Grand Rapids. The Forest History Center there has recreated a 1900's logging camp. At the Blandin Paper Company, visitors can watch paper being made. Each August, the town hosts Tall Timber Days. Lumberjacks compete in tree-chopping and pole-climbing contests. West of town is the Chippewa National Forest.

Itasca State Park is west of the forest. It is a good place to end a tour of Minnesota. The park was founded in 1891. That makes it Minnesota's oldest state park. Lake Itasca is in the park. The Mississippi River begins at that lake. There, young children can wade across the river. It is only a few inches deep and a few feet wide.

Lake Itasca, where the Mississippi River begins

A Gallery of Famous Minnesotans

A Gallery of Famous Minnesotans

Many famous Americans have been Minnesotans. They include authors, athletes, Supreme Court justices, and vice presidents.

James J. Hill (1838-1916) was born in Canada. He came to St. Paul when he was eighteen. There he founded the Great Northern Railway. The line ran from Duluth to Seattle, Washington. Hill also owned steamships and iron and coal mines.

DeWitt Wallace (1889-1981) was born in St. Paul. He founded *Reader's Digest*. It became one of the world's most popular magazines.

Roy Wilkins (1901-1981) was born in Missouri. He grew up in St. Paul. Wilkins became a great black leader. He helped organize the 1963 March on Washington for civil rights. Wilkins served as head of the National Association for the Advancement of Colored People (1965-1977). "Mr. Civil Rights" also won the Presidential Medal of Freedom.

Four Minnesotans have served on the U.S. Supreme Court. **Pierce Butler** (1866-1939) was born near Northfield. He served on the country's

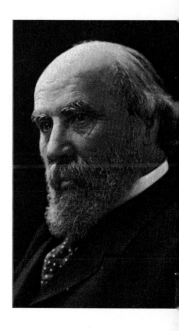

James J. Hill (above) was called the "Empire Builder" because he built railroads across the American frontier.

Opposite: Supreme Court Justice William O. Douglas

highest court from 1923 to 1939. **William O. Douglas** (1898-1980) was born in Maine, Minnesota. He served the longest of any Supreme Court justice (1939-1975). Douglas supported the rights of the poor and the powerless. **Warren Burger** was born in St. Paul in 1907. **Harry Blackmun** was born in Illinois in 1908. But Blackmun grew up in St. Paul. Burger and Blackmun became best friends. They played tennis and delivered newspapers together. Later, they served on the Supreme Court with Douglas. Burger was chief justice (1969-1986). Blackmun was an associate justice (1970-1994).

Minnesota has also had famous U.S. senators. Some have become U.S. vice presidents and run for president. **Hubert Humphrey** (1911-1978) was born in South Dakota. He graduated from the University of Minnesota. In 1945, he was elected mayor of Minneapolis. The year before, he helped join the Farmer-Labor party with the Democratic party. The new party has been known as the Democratic-Farmer-Labor (DFL) party. In 1948, he became Minnesota's first Democrat elected to the U.S. Senate. There, he helped start the Peace Corps. Later, he served as vice president (1965-1969) under President Lyndon Johnson. In 1968, he ran for president but lost to Richard Nixon.

Hubert Humphrey

Eugene McCarthy was born in 1916 in Watkins. He also served Minnesota in the U.S. Senate (1959- 1971). In 1968, McCarthy called for an end to the Vietnam War. He began a campaign for president of the United States. McCarthy battled Humphrey to be the Democratic party's presidential candidate. McCarthy lost.

Walter Mondale

Walter Mondale was born in Ceylon, Minnesota, in 1928. He too became a Democratic U.S. senator from Minnesota (1964-1977). Mondale helped pass the Civil Rights Act of 1968. Later, he was vice president (1977-1981) under President Jimmy Carter. In 1984, Mondale ran for president against President Ronald Reagan. Reagan

Left: Artist Leslie C. Kouba
Right Sculptor Paul Manship

won reelection. In 1993, President Bill Clinton appointed Mondale ambassador to Japan.

Elaine Stately (1937-1988) was born on Minnesota's White Earth Indian Reservation. She was an Ojibway. Stately helped found the American Indian Movement. It works for American Indian rights in the United States and Canada. Stately also began the Native American Olympics.

Sculptor **Paul Manship** (1885-1966) was born in St. Paul. His *Indian Hunter with Dog* is a bronze sculpture. It is part of a St. Paul fountain. Artist **Les Kouba** was born in Hutchinson in 1917. He sold his first painting at the age of eleven. Kouba is known for his wildlife paintings.

Minnesota has a gift for producing authors. **Ole Rölvaag** (1876-1931) was born in Norway. He taught Norwegian at St. Olaf College in Northfield (1906-1931). Rölvaag also wrote novels. *Giants in the Earth* is about Norwegian pioneers in Minnesota.

Wanda Gág (1893-1946) was born in New Ulm. She was the oldest of seven children. Gág helped support her family. At first, she wrote stories and drew pictures for a newspaper. Later, Gág became a children's book author and illustrator. *Millions of Cats* (1928) is her best-known work.

Sinclair Lewis (1885-1951) was born in Sauk Centre. His 1920 novel *Main Street* was about small-

Left: Wanda Gág Right: Sinclair Lewis with his wife Dorothy Thompson In 1930, Sinclair Lewis became the first American to win the Nobel Prize for literature.

Playwright August Wilson

Left: F. Scott Fitzgerald with his wife Zelda and daughter Scotty Right: Judy Garland in her role as Dorothy in The Wizard of Oz

town America. It made him famous. **F. Scott Fitzgerald** (1896-1940) was born in St. Paul. He wrote about rich Americans and their lack of values. His best-known work is *The Great Gatsby*. "The Ice Palace" and "Winter Dreams" are two of his short stories. They are set in Minnesota.

August Wilson was born in Pennsylvania in 1945. Later, he moved to the Twin Cities area to write. In 1968, Wilson founded the Black Horizons Theater Company in St. Paul. Wilson writes plays about everyday black people. *Fences* and *The Piano Lesson* won Pulitzer Prizes for drama.

Judy Garland (1922-1969) was born in Grand Rapids. She became a famous singer and movie star. In 1939, Garland played Dorothy in *The Wizard of*

Musician Bob Dylan (facing the camera)

Oz. Her later movies included *Meet Me in St. Louis* and *Easter Parade.* She sang in all of them. **Jessica Lange** was born in Cloquet in 1949. She won the 1982 Academy Award for Best Supporting Actress. It was for her role in *Tootsie.* **Winona Ryder** was born in 1971. Her name is the same as her Minnesota birthplace. Ryder had important roles in *Edward Scissorshands* and *Mermaids.*

Bob Dylan was born Robert Zimmerman in Duluth in 1941. He became a songwriter and singer. Dylan's songs include "Blowin' in the Wind" and "The Times They Are A-Changin'." **Prince Rogers Nelson** was born in Minneapolis in 1958. Prince became a famous rock star. His *Purple Rain*

When Charles Schulz (above) was a baby, his father nicknamed him after a cartoon racehorse, "Sparky."

Garrison Keillor

album has sold over 10 million copies. Prince's recording studio is in the Minneapolis area.

Charles Schulz was born in Minneapolis in 1922. He published his first drawing when he was fifteen. He created the "Peanuts" cartoon in 1950. Today, it appears in 2,300 newspapers in sixty-eight countries.

Garrison Keillor was born in 1942 in Anoka. He hosted a popular radio show, "A Prairie Home Companion." He told stories of Lake Wobegon, an imaginary town much like Keillor's birthplace.

Charles Bender (1883-1954) was born on the White Earth Indian Reservation. He became a great pitcher. In 1953, Bender was elected to the Baseball Hall of Fame. **Dave Winfield** was born in St. Paul in 1951. He also became a baseball star. Winfield played in twelve straight All-Star Games.

Patty Berg was born in Minneapolis in 1918. She won eighty-three golf tournaments between 1935 and 1981. They included the first U.S. Women's Open Championship in 1946.

Alan Page was born in Ohio in 1945. He graduated from the University of Minnesota Law School. At the same time, he played for the Minnesota Vikings. In 1992, Page became Minnesota's first black state Supreme Court judge.

Ann Bancroft was born in St. Paul in 1955. In 1986, she spent fifty-six days walking 550 miles to the North Pole. In 1992-93, Bancroft skied 1,700 miles to the South Pole. This teacher was the first woman to reach both poles on foot.

Left: One-time football star Alan Page in 1992 became Minnesota's first black state Supreme Court judge.
Right: Professional golfer Patty Berg

The birthplace of Ann Bancroft, Charles Schulz, Judy Garland, and Walter Mondale . . .

Home, too, of James J. Hill, Hubert Humphrey, Alan Page, and Ole Rölvaag . . .

The Land of Sky-Blue Waters where waterskiing and snowmobiling began . . .

Today, the top state at mining iron ore and growing sugar beets . . .

This is the Gopher State—Minnesota!

Did You Know?

What may have been the greatest logjam in history occurred on the St. Croix River near Taylors Falls in 1886. It took 200 men six weeks to break up the 2-mile jam.

Minnesota is known for its severe weather. In November 1940, fifty-three people died during a blizzard. An April 1886 tornado in the St. Cloud area killed seventy-four people.

Charles Schulz's drawings of Charlie Brown and friends are beloved around the world. Yet, in art school, Schulz's worst grade was for a lesson on drawing children.

The Mall of America opened in Bloomington in 1992. It is the largest shopping and entertainment complex in the United States. The mall has more than 400 stores, 14 movie theaters, and nearly 50 restaurants.

Cuyler Adams discovered iron ore in the Cuyuna Range. He named the range by joining *Cuy* from his first name with *Una,* his dog's name, to create *Cuyuna.*

A town near the Twin Cities was named Florence in honor of the founder's daughter. But when the settlers learned that there was another Florence, Minnesota, they renamed their town Young America. Sleepy Eye and Welcome are two other Minnesota towns with unusual names.

William and Roger Christian are from Warroad, Minnesota. The Christian brothers were on the 1960 U.S. Olympic team that won the gold medal in hockey. William's son David played on the 1980 gold-medal-winning team.

Each year about 2 million Minnesota trees become Christmas trees.

The St. Paul Winter Carnival, begun in 1886, is the nation's oldest winter festival. There are speed-skating and ice-carving contests. Softball is played on ice. In some years, an ice palace is built. The 1992 palace was the tallest structure ever made of ice. It stood 167 feet high. That is over sixteen stories!

In-line skates were invented in the early 1980s by the Olson brothers, Scott and Brennan, of Minneapolis.

Minnesotans are healthy, well-educated, and active in politics. Minnesotans live to an average age of seventy-six. Only Hawaiians live longer. Nine out of ten are high-school graduates. Only Vermont has more. One of five has a college degree. Eight out of ten are registered to vote. Only North Dakota has a higher percentage of voters.

55

Minnesota Information

State flag

Lady's slipper

Common loon

Area: 84,402 square miles (the twelfth-biggest state)

Greatest Distance North to South: 407 miles

Greatest Distance East to West: 360 miles

Borders: The country of Canada to the north; Lake Superior and Wisconsin to the east; Iowa to the south; North Dakota and South Dakota to the west

Highest Point: Eagle Mountain (2,301 feet above sea level)

Lowest Point: 602 feet above sea level, along Lake Superior

Hottest Recorded Temperature: 114° F. (at Beardsley on July 29, 1917, and at Moorhead on July 6, 1936)

Coldest Recorded Temperature: -59° F. (at Leech Lake Dam on February 9, 1899, and at Pokegama Falls on February 16, 1903)

Statehood: The thirty-second state, on May 11, 1858

Origin of Name: *Minnesota* comes from two Dakota Indian words meaning "cloud-reflecting water"

Capital: St. Paul

Counties: 87

United States Representatives: 8

State Senators: 67

State Representatives: 134

State Song: "Hail! Minnesota," by Truman E. Rickard and Arthur E. Upson

State Motto: *L'Etoile du Nord*, French meaning "The Star of the North"

Nicknames: "Gopher State," "North Star State," "Land of 10,000 Lakes," "Land of Sky-Blue Waters," "Bread and Butter State"

State Seal: Adopted in 1861

State Flag: Adopted in 1957

State Bird: Common loon

State Mushroom: Morel

State Grain: Wild rice

State Flower: Pink and white lady's slipper

State Gemstone: Lake Superior agate

Some Rivers: Mississippi, Minnesota, St. Croix, Red, St. Louis, Crow Wing

Some Lakes: Red, Mille Lacs, Leech, Winnibigoshish, Minnetonka, Vermilion, Pepin, and Stone

Wildlife: White-tailed deer, black bears, moose, timber wolves, bobcats, foxes, otters, badgers, woodchucks, weasels, gophers, muskrats, minks, bats, turtles, common loons, ducks, bald eagles, owls, sparrows, pheasants, woodpeckers

Fishing Products: Walleyed pike, northern pike, lake herring, catfish, whitefish, muskellunges, bass, crappies

Manufactured Products: Computers, tractors, construction machinery, breakfast cereals and other foods, heart valves and other medical supplies, lumber, wood and paper products, adhesive tape, books

Farm Products: Hogs, turkeys, milk, eggs, beef cattle, sugar beets, oats, soybeans, barley, corn, hay, wheat, apples, potatoes, peas

Mining Products: Iron ore, clay, sand and gravel, granite, limestone

Population: 4,375,099, twentieth among the fifty states (1990 U.S. Census Bureau figures)

Major Cities (1990 Census):

Minneapolis	368,383	Brooklyn Park	56,381
St. Paul	272,235	Coon Rapids	52,978
Bloomington	86,335	Burnsville	51,288
Duluth	85,493	Plymouth	50,889
Rochester	70,745	St. Cloud	48,812

State Tree: Norway pine

State Fish: Walleyed pike

State Drink: Milk

Norway pine

Lake Superior agates

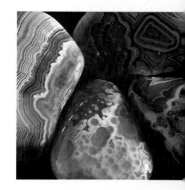

Morel mushrooms

MINNESOTA HISTORY

Daniel Greysolon, Sieur Du Luth, explored Minnesota and claimed it for France.

10,000 B.C.—American Indians reach Minnesota

About 1660—French traders Pierre Radisson and Médard Chouart, Sieur des Groseilliers, reach Minnesota

1679—Daniel Greysolon, Sieur Du Luth, explores Minnesota and claims it for France

1680—Father Louis Hennepin sees and names the Falls of St. Anthony in what is now Minneapolis

1695—Pierre le Sueur builds a post near what is now Red Wing

1762—France gives Minnesota land west of the Mississippi River to Spain

1763—France loses Minnesota land east of the Mississippi to England

1783—England loses its land east of the Mississippi, including Minnesota, to the United States

1800—France regains control of Minnesota west of the Mississippi

1803—France sells a huge tract of land, including western Minnesota, to the United States, which now owns all of Minnesota

1819—Fort Snelling is begun at the mouth of the Minnesota, south of what is now Minneapolis

1832—Henry Schoolcraft discovers Lake Itasca, the source of the Mississippi River

1838—Minneapolis and St. Paul are begun

1849—Congress establishes the Minnesota Territory; the *Minnesota Pioneer*, Minnesota's first newspaper, is issued at St. Paul

1851—The Dakota give up large areas of land in Minnesota

1858—Minnesota becomes the thirty-second state on May 11

1861—About 22,000 Minnesotans help the North win the Civil War

1862—In August-September, about 500 settlers are killed during the Dakota wars; in December, thirty-eight Indians are hanged for their part in the uprising

1869—The University of Minnesota opens as a four-year college

1889—The Mayo Clinic is begun in Rochester

1890—The Merritt brothers find iron ore in the Mesabi Range

1894—The Great Hinckley Fire kills more than 400 people

1917-18—Over 123,000 Minnesotans help win World War I

1918—Minnesota's Farmer-Labor party is begun

1928—Minnesotan Frank Billings Kellogg helps write the Kellogg-Briand Peace Pact, which attempts to outlaw war

1929-39—The Great Depression hurts Minnesota mining, manufacturing, and farming

1941-45—About 325,000 Minnesotans help win World War II

1955—The country's first big plant for processing iron ore from taconite opens at Silver Bay

1958—Happy 100th birthday, state of Minnesota!

1965—Minnesotan Hubert Humphrey becomes vice president of the United States

1969—Minnesotan Warren Burger becomes chief justice of the U.S. Supreme Court

1977—Minnesotan Walter Mondale becomes vice president of the United States

1987—Minnesota begins a school-choice program; "Second Chance" begins to bring dropouts back to high school; the Minnesota Twins win the World Series

1990—The Gopher State's population is 4,375,099

1991—The Minnesota Twins again win the World Series

1992—Minnesota pioneers a health-insurance program to help the poor and jobless

1993—Fifty-four women are sworn in as members of the state legislature

Lewis H. Merritt (center) and his brothers found iron ore in the Mesabi Range around 1890.

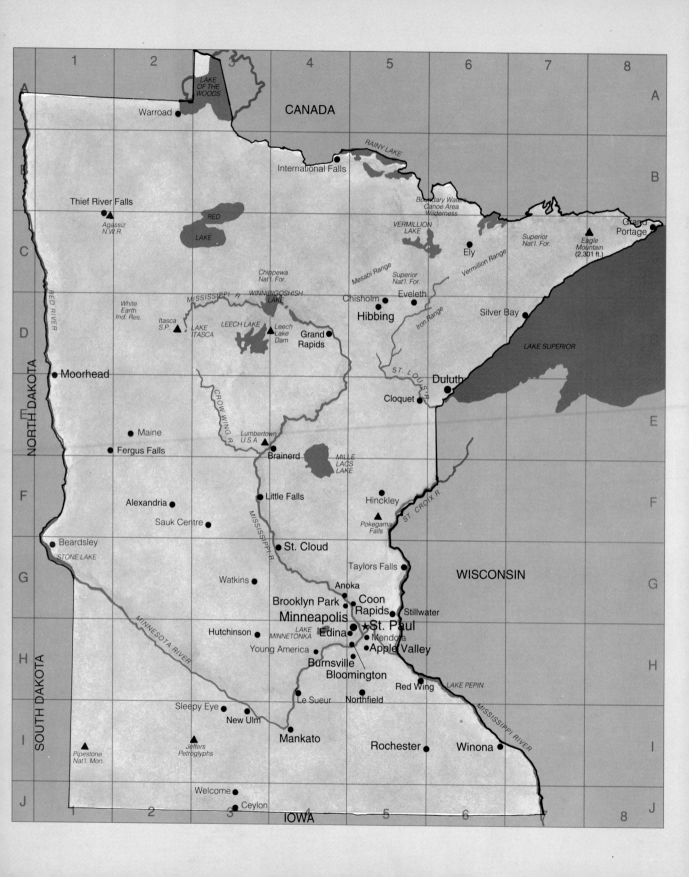

MAP KEY

Agassiz National Wildlife Refuge	C1
Alexandria	F2
Anoka	G4
Apple Valley	H5
Beardsley	G1
Bloomington	H5
Boundary Waters Canoe Area Wilderness	B5,6
Brainerd	E4
Brooklyn Park	G4
Burnsville	H4
Ceylon	J3
Chippewa National Forest	C3,4
Chisholm	D5
Cloquet	E5
Coon Rapids	G5
Crow Wing River	E3
Duluth	E6
Eagle Mountain	C7
Edina	H4
Ely	C6
Eveleth	D5
Fergus Falls	E2
Grand Portage	C8
Grand Rapids	D4
Hibbing	D5
Hinckley	F5
Hutchinson	H3
International Falls	B4
Iron Range	D5,6
Itasca State Park	D2
Jeffers Petroglyphs	I3
Lake Itasca	D2
Lake Minnetonka	H4
Lake of the Woods	A3
Lake Pepin	H6
Lake Superior	D7
Leech Lake	D3
Leech Lake Dam	D4
Le Sueur	H4
Little Falls	F3
Lumbertown U.S.A.	E3
Maine	E2
Mankato	I4
Mendota	H5
Mesabi Range	C5
Mille Lacs Lake	E,F4
Minneapolis	G4
Minnesota River	H2
Mississippi River	F,G3;I6,7
Moorhead	E1
New Ulm	I3
Northfield	H5
Pipestone National Monument	I1
Pokegama Falls	F5
Rainy Lake	B5
Red Lake	C3
Red River	D1
Red Wing	H6
Rochester	I5
St. Cloud	G4
St. Croix River	F5,6
St. Louis River	D,E5
St. Paul	H5
Sauk Centre	F3
Silver Bay	D7
Sleepy Eye	I3
Stillwater	G5
Stone Lake	G1
Superior National Forest	C5,7
Taylors Falls	G5
Thief River Falls	B1
Vermilion Lake	C5
Vermilion Range	C6
Warroad	A2
Watkins	G3
Welcome	J3
White Earth Indian Reservation	D2
Winnibigoshish Lake	D3,4
Winona	I6
Young America	H4

GLOSSARY

ancient: Related to a time long ago

blizzard: A snowstorm driven by high winds

capital: The city that is the seat of government

capitol: The building in which the government meets

civil rights: The rights of a citizen

climate: The typical weather of a region

depression: Hard times with widespread joblessness

explore: To visit and study an unknown land

glacier: A mass of slowly moving ice

mammoths and mastodons: Elephantlike animals that no longer exist

million: A thousand thousand (1,000,000)

petroglyph: A rock carving

plains: Rather flat lands

pollution: Waste that dirties the air, land, and water

population: The number of people in a place

powwow: A get-together of American Indians

replica: A life-size copy

reservation (Indian): Lands in the United States that are set aside for American Indians

taconite: A rock that contains low-grade iron ore

tepee: A cone-shaped tent made by North American Indians

territory: Land owned by a country

tornado: A powerful windstorm that comes from a whirling, funnel-shaped cloud

transportation: The process of moving people and things

voyageur: A person who carried goods by canoe for a fur company

wigwam: A rounded Indian home made of wood and bark

wildlife refuge: A place where animals are protected

PICTURE ACKNOWLEDGMENTS

Front cover, © R. Kord/**H. Armstrong Roberts;** 1, © Andy Sacks/**Tony Stone Images, Inc.;** 2, **Tom Dunnington;** 3, © **Greg Ryan/Sally Beyer;** 5, **Tom Dunnington;** 6-7, © Terry Donnelly/**Tom Stack and Associates;** 9 (left), © Ron Goulet/**Dembinsky Photo Assoc.;** 9 (right), **Courtesy of Hammond Incorporated, Maplewood, New Jersey;** 10 (top), © **Tom Till;** 10 (bottom), © Carl R. Sams, II/**Dembinsky Photo Assoc.;** 11, © Greg Ryan/**Sally Beyer;** 12-13, **Minnesota Historical Society, photo by Oscar L. Pederson;** 14, © **Tom Till;** 15 (top), **The Bettmann Archive;** 15 (bottom), © **Virginia R. Grimes;** 16, **Buffalo Bill Historical Center, Cody, Wy., Gift of Mrs. Karl Frank;** 17, © **James P. Rowan;** 18 (top), © **James P. Rowan;** 18 (bottom), **Minnesota Historical Society;** 20, **Minnesota Historical Society, Photo by W. H. Illingworth;** 21, **North Wind Picture Archives;** 22, **The Bettmann Archive;** 23, **Minnesota Historical Society;** 24, **Minnesota Historical Society;** 25, © **Cameramann International, Ltd.;** 26, © Mark E. Gibson/**mga/Photri;** 27 (top), © Cleo Freelance Photo/**N E Stock Photo;** 27 (bottom), © Don Hamerman/**N E Stock Photo;** 28 (top), © **Minnesota Office of Tourism;** 28 (bottom), © Don Hamerman/**N E Stock Photo;** 29, © **Cameramann International, Ltd.;** 30-31, © Raymond Barnes/**Tony Stone Images, Inc.;** 33 (both pictures), © R. Kord/**H. Armstrong Roberts;** 34 (top), © Michael Ma Po Shum/**Tony Stone Images;** 34 (bottom), © Greg Rayn/**Sally Beyer;** 35 (both pictures), © **Greg Ryan/Sally Beyer;** 36 (top), © Roger Bickel/**N E Stock Photo;** 36 (bottom), © Scott Berner/**mga/Photri;** 38, © **Cameramann International, Ltd.;** 39 (top), © **Cameramann International, Ltd.;** 39 (bottom), © **P. Michael Whye;** 40, © **Cameramann International, Ltd.;** 41, © Raymond G. Barnes/**Tony Stone Images, Inc.;** 42 (top), © **Cameramann International, Ltd.;** 42 (bottom), © **Greg Ryan/Sally Beyer;** 43, © Maxwell Mackenzie/**Tony Stone Images, Inc.;** 44, **Artist Bruno Beran/ photographer Vic Boswell, National Geographic Society/Collection of the Supreme Court of the United States;** 45, **Stock Montage, Inc.;** 46 (both pictures), **Stock Montage, Inc.;** 47 (both pictures), **AP/Wide World Photos;** 48 (left), **Minnesota Historical Society;** 48 (right), **AP/Wide World Photos;** 49 (left), **Minnesota Historical Society;** 49 (right), **Stock Montage, Inc.;** 50 (all pictures), **AP/Wide World Photos;** 51, **AP/Wide World Photos;** 52 (both pictures), **AP/Wide World Photos;** 53 (both pictures), **AP/Wide World Photos;** 54 (top), © R. Kord/ **H. Armstrong Roberts;** 55 (top left and top right), **Courtesy Rollerblade, Inc.;** 55 (bottom), **Minnesota Office of Tourism;** 56 (top), **Courtesy Flag Research Center, Winchester, Massachusetts 01890;** 56 (middle), © Conrad A. Gutraj/**Root Resources;** 56 (bottom), © **Lynn M. Stone;** 57 (top), © **Jerry Hennen;** 57 (middle), © Louise K. Broman/ **Root Resources;** 57 (bottom), © Kouhout Productions/**Root Resources;** 58, **Minnesota Historical Society;** 59, **Minnesota Historical Society;** 60, **Tom Dunnington;** back cover, © Terry Donnelly/**Tom Stack and Associates**

INDEX

Page numbers in boldface type indicate illustrations.

ABOUT THE AUTHORS

Dennis and Judith Fradin have coauthored several books in the From Sea to Shining Sea series. The Fradins both graduated from Northwestern University in 1967. Dennis has been a professional writer for twenty years, and has published 150 books. His works for Childrens Press include the Young People's Stories of Our States series, the Disaster! series, and the Thirteen Colonies series. Judith earned her M.A. in literature from Northwestern University and taught high-school and college English for many years. The Fradins, who are the parents of Anthony, Diana, and Michael, live in Evanston, Illinois.